T0160841

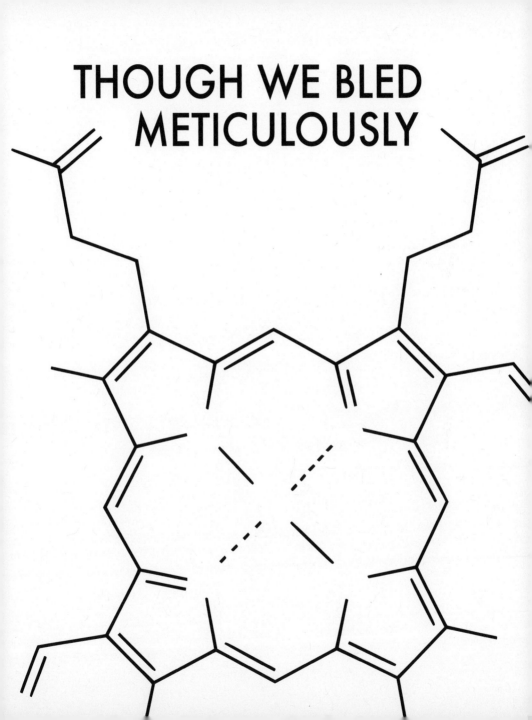

Though We Bled Meticulously

Josh Fomon

Black Ocean
Boston · Detroit · Chicago

Black Ocean
P.O. Box 52030
Boston, MA 02205
blackocean.org

Cover Design by Janaka Stucky | janakastucky.com
Book Design by Nikkita Cohoon | nikkita.co

ISBN 978-1-939568-1-68

Library of Congress Cataloging-in-Publication Data

Names: Fomon, Josh, 1987- author.
Title: Though we bled meticulously / Josh Fomon.
Description: Boston : Black Ocean, [2016]
Identifiers: LCCN 2016006593 | ISBN 9781939568168
Classification: LCC PS3606.O55 A6 2016 | DDC 811/.6-dc23
LC record available at http://lccn.loc.gov/2016006593

FIRST EDITION

for Dave, Kari, and Kristin

Subversion is the very movement of writing: the very movement of death.

The written page is no mirror. To write means to confront an unknown face.

Driven mad, the sea, unable to die in a single wave.

—Edmond Jabès

THOUGH WE BLED
METICULOUSLY

‡

And the energy
was spoken painted upon

        the page. We changed our flocks
    began to quiver.

      We took our fields and
buried them from fire.

The flotsam destruction jar
        —there were many slaughters
    many containments.

We could   not help.
We could not   recollect our heaven.
      The world would not   look up

to feel the uncurling   of skin.

‡

        The pastured throat not   furtive
all the bonesack   what I yell
subsumes

                    in deep collapse.

‡

We have faith in the dark

as we mark the chase.

We suffer

callous for the chance   to exist elsewhere.

Our possibility lifts us.
            The page is a certain perimeter full

of an inconsistent rage   a malfunction

in sight. When we opened   to another language

we found the drooping   prayers

like a wet book   overspilt of ink.

We narrowed our salve   compressed
            what we could   in our selves.

Outlined our bodies   in what could be bled
            from the containment.

‡

Intensely morning   this face in the broken

fire—the harsh portrait of words

    smashing. How will the air receive
      our crumbling?

I spent the entirety of my youth ministering to my open sores.
The grid underneath my skin maps a breath in motioned
time. Pulsar invariable. The stray passenger between lives and
people—beginning to drone. Wet, dark warm. It was all flowers
blooming in the veins. Pure quadrants of direction—solstice of
orogeny. I connected my selves to other selves and the dark
things they do. It was here between the arts I took my first bride
and buried my vows in my forearm. The state had formed under
my breath through my eyes—the world brightened in sharp
drowning noise. I tongued through the air a green moisture
in her aroma. She took my shadow and left me disconnected
to the feet I had compassed. Errant erratic. Exact aperture of
misunderstanding. I pled constantly to save my life.

Across the sky as the broad sword on fire.

    To have a culpability. The dirty calm
  striations. The sun hue struck

    wisps in clouds. I had learned how to mouth my name.

      Call this a way out.

‡

(I could be a resilient   silence. The hidden self

where there are no faces.   Never misplace the future
                                the space it once

inhabited. The void we left   gravity as whole regions—juicy.

                Pushed to an infinity an instant
        will exist forever   resonating away

                                from a climax
                                of resolve.

She had begun to teach me how to bend
                        an infinity together   one whole

                precipice to my creation. To what I could drop in).

‡

How will I know the howling?
        Breadth as sensation. The earnest attempt

      to shape a remedy. My hands   are something

to worry about.   See how they create this history?
    A peninsula beyond the aching of faith.

    Watch now the embroidery of direction

    the maps of ligaments and cold   distance.

         From a position in the air
    the necrotized detritus
          patterned in June. Follow my close

scorched liminally   scorched sooth

    ink assured of its power   a swagger of permanence

    of knowing the threat of crumbling

and worse yet.

‡

(In the memory   light against the window
    stuck and peeling flowers' simulacra.
         Blood the plot   these hands toil

outward for life. We are like an ossuary gilded

       to understand a history   of wreckage.
         In my hands I can feel   the failings
          and recoveries.

I have found a break   to escape devotion).

      And quieter still
    the wreckage of its collapse.

The faith in gravity

     when the weeks molder—
silence a mark

of exigency and evolution—can there
only be me.

9

‡

                        Glacial   the
                slow turning smelt in lime—
                fossils intricately tinctured
                enervated   not
                immediately we bond the
                bawl   together   I
                in my
                        kinds   imposed
                breakdowns in recorded
                acts of subversion.

here stillfooted   assured of assuaging hands—

in their place a blackhole   a consumption of what we once held.
                        I in my we am   beginning to sculpt
                        a certain love in experience.

            Listen. Form the oceans under nails. Form the dirt
                        from perfect resonance.
            Listen to the thundering infinity
        the eve we said no more.

Blued and rifling   my mouth

waiting for a song to appear.

‡

(hibernal the costs of lucid blue
the cracking sheets from that night on orange
wilted flowers across orange thin dust
(I remember because I was young
the kindness of two heroes
falling black across a vivid sky made more vivid
(dust covering their bodies)
the quick pooling of light slowly through the air
a drop of water becomes orange)
(orange as the plain on which my eyes disfigure a memory)
if the sky unto itself were pictured as a symphony)

‡

But the next day the wine, ideally shaped, was intense and very warm too
plain (in its idea).
if it's not pictured like a frame
that could be held like a poem.
over a plate of rice
(stains even on Sunday)
the shift of position held

holding her head perfectly
of image and time of day

as when she wasn't there.

Incredulous, the disbelief
(So what if it's Sunday?)
The feeling I get brooding
for it, a shock-coffee study,
narrations (brilliantly shadowed
stationed like an island, that ever
(the watcher situated above
distanced from the representation
imagines a protocol of morning)
Sonora orange, shadows livid

‡

Thunderous pause:
shadows galloping, forming themselves before mustangs.

I refused to march along—their pace had not yet set in winter, the infernal
blossom clogging the drainage. She was lost in context—(she tore slowly)
a borderless hoard of faceless people trying to stoke the ineffable.

‡

My partition of pagination left me
torn and unable to tear the composition
to cast upon
a thickness) the page clumped
in spite of the noise

in her dimension

(she blacks out in a field)
covered in purpose
on the surface I cast the shape of a flower with cutouts of
dimensional atrophy like a tree poised to fall
orange like the blue that made it vivid.

onto the whiteness of nothing.
stained orange like nothing orange.

typography
a wall (the book unyielding in its stolid state
to create depth in its wrinkle—
the blossomed clog unfurled
upon the page.   She should feel free
to inhabit fully the margins pushed to exhale
yet I cannot persuade a passion
boundless order I say
to be held like depth
words and intricate missing utterances
unable to cast upon a symmetry

A whorl fading
Its borders

‡

Points of Interest:

h. *to think and think and think and think and think...*

w. when there is demand   i write   no demand   i write

e. distracted by distrust   trussed   in words

a. hold our sway, our constant spinning

r. OOOOoooooo~~~~line of symmetry~~~~OOOOoooooo

e. i transform   for you   means   something

z. marred with notion   of completion   or lack thereof

13. fail, duck through

h. *to think and think and think and think and think...*

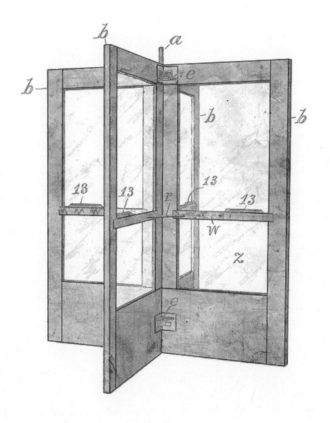

‡

And then I turned back

    the untenable

eclipse worn without   an afternoon proper.

    Eloquence and fevered   melodious breath.

        Let me soak here

     in the warm pleasures

  thresholds cannot sing.

‡

There is a name for children

       when they realize

they are repositories   of their own existence.

       We become flustered   knowing

       the pull we feel when it's near.

We feel the electric silence

      fragile sigh of high

      frequencies the mellow red   in the corners of eyes.

‡

To have fervored the break
　　　　my arms contain　　　all that I am.

　　Beyond small unwinding　　　we believe separation

is a colder day.　　The bleak fog
　　　　　　　speaks.　　　Fortune

like wood on a stick.　　The dalliance began to simmer

　　　　the colors began to hue negligence　　　and terror.
　　　　When we engendered

　　this energy　　　　　　trauma ignited another

　　　　nature　　　　time slowed　　into an almost
　　　　　　　　　　　　　　　　instant.

The spring exploded in late

　snow. If we were to reach out　　　we could articulate a drift.
　　　Like a painter bound forever to panel containment

we cannot escape our limbs
　　　　we cannot sever the extension　　beyond them.

‡

I detain my prayers   we are dwindling youth.

The riddles scattered in tears
parenthetical to capture that
creature. My heart is a place to
fracture and sustain translations
outgrowing meaning what I
want. In a bed of stars it is so
easy to look down and forget
our leisure. What I need is a
reckoning. An ache to need what
we are welling up in forgotten
organs. Let me grope my sheets
until sleep is forgotten.

How do we survive   a scrutiny a vigilance of the incommunicable?

Chaos and fortune
the intersection where I outlast. We forget
the bombs buried there.

We are beginning   in sleep.

‡

Dear We

The lake of lilies
          still has a sense
of shining in
moments of crisis.
Perhaps that's why
          the immigrants settled
here ages ago.
It's a contraption
          so immense

it goes unnoticed
in its power.

                              Let's pretend an industry
                                   contains the waves
                              that once winnowed
                              a field

of confarreation,
          I have learned
alternative
hazards

                        may be
circumvented, tied
            in
a rippling layer
            where the world
separates in human,
                        constantly awakening
                        an utterance of deep
                        death.

Ruins
on the side of the bank
            the flock digs
into an appetite—
what goes unanswered
            alive.
                        Rejuvenation happily
burns.

‡

Yes, I have lost
the axial proportions
to my life—it takes

a season to rot
a leaf from the roots.

‡

I never called off
never spoke
to calm a storm

                    from my deliberate

                            blossoming
                    and the life cut from.

If the outcome
        of life becomes
conscious
the lake laps.
Always pulling.

Always pulling
        as if the leaves
change constantly
an absence.

‡

Hold on

        centrifugal creation

your eyes truly reflect
                fountaining their observance

of stars.

‡

Hold on

      centrifugal pact
      fuse of shadow
            to skin.

          As a centrifugal self
          is this how we become?

We wept spooling lovers
          swept them galaxies away.

          They fought for time   the stasis centrifugal
      they fled until they could not see
      each other.

The absence in motion

      a brilliant powdered architecture

          in the fossils I once moved

through.

          We once were instantly twilight

instantly bricks.

‡

Lips numb from genesis.

Traveled yew-wise this pattern-dawned spectacle.

    The birth of people
        into new shades of rising sun.

Why the way back is perusal and shame.

‡

The arousal of I in spectacular setting

the vista wavered
                            in purposeful nothing.

            Water lapidary crystalline
        against my washing body.
I became—
            the aft of my totem   my outward creation

        the urgency to be halved yet brimmed blue at the touch.

        I could not find my motion   my congruence in landscape.

        Explosions mimicked galaxies in the sky.
                Inside an efference   an insurgency to capture why.

This wheel narrowing yet held

strange. I traveled across the moon

        setting. I could not move an inch.

           The preternatural
feast in your fettering palm.

          Come here and glisten.

    Yet still the deer stare
       through my eyes.

‡

Extinguished around the neck
      the knife shimmering as we carved

a history in the field.

          The bees will remember always
the looks on our faces

planets of unreachable flesh.

         A lone couple passing
along our ribs murmurs quietly

what leaves fettered.

We howled if the voice passed.

            If veiled we whispered
toward the moon.

‡

to have extrapolated space (   )/and caused a raucous (scene—a cure/
extracted) mote in fractious face,/appropriated proper lure,/and spoke
(   ) of tragic words erased—/misconception as taut allure.

obsession: write (*possess, plunder,*)/the action marred with feeling,
hope—/to model risk (aversion per)/the body's marks and scars—the
rope/purveying   loss torn asunder—/(we need e'er a spasmodic
trope)

i think i tried to kill, with noose,/my poetry, perused what dripped/off,
licked it with (my) tongue: found use/dilapidated, full (and) lipped,/its
present   (state) void of misuse—/its space open   ( ) (frayed and
ripped).

Our doors perceive our actions (   ) a threshold of completion or
conceded failure—to forget is to flail.

‡

                                    That would not
                              would the harbinger
                              in a raster of silence.

          We said we were splitting,
                              trepidating like bones.
                    Through ribs the pain   remains

                    swift   weather wrought against

                              the moaning—curvature
          taken to awake—
                              manic abrogation.

(Yet torqued—)

our contour—loins   turned down
            slight of twist—to have created

            rotation. No more a mask
    No more the ground to   trudge.

                We must be implicit.
                We must stop—

                        Prepare yourself to flee

                                    to say

            you need saving.

‡

Tawdry nothing, that hole

‡

Twilight incandescence
unfastened.

An infinity we are just beginning
to comprehend
we cannot.

As if all at once
we blinked.

‡

Godhead impediment, there is me, conscious, subdued plenary heart. Elsewhere was splayed stellar, moments when I was supernova—spreading distance above you. I could only muster witness. Had to practice fading, daily. Between deaths I am me, ever detached, Swami Now, frankly blank, demon-eyed. Miscreant, my place, material body. Demonstrating itinerant trajectory. The story of fleeing everything near and fearing its birth into dead bodies. If to be able to tolerate liberation, urges attained in deriving you a thousand times, I am a caller of your faith.

          It becomes
     difficult to breathe
               in large swaths   of living,
                       to articulate the sway of branches

               when a fire   divines a mouth
                into the swarm, the lingering
   apocalypse tearing itself   from the breach.

                  Yesterday, I crossed another planet.
          Crossed another sunsetting.
            This analog is another lie.

Lord, because of this constant elocution, because of this constant execution, lord, I am beginning to touch a great death. Beginning to feel barbed, what exists to be observed and never touched, a mending so obscure as to wade into nothing pure, a being plural like waves to moon—never ceased, never reached.

Secluded conqueror, o how you abandon, o how your goddess melts me, my many puffed-up perversions, my gazing testimony of everything at a distance. Let me surrender. Stage greater contaminations. Science is enough to keep me curious.

Profuse goddess, charge of cooperation, contemplate lust. Symptoms merge into one mending. Who speaks outward from a void, whose mind? Enough is farther disturbed, fixed to communion with fountained serenity—come in Saturday, fool, discoverer, ancient of all that can be lost.

That we were not promised

what we looked like
under the wind—
soft-lipped, becoming,

a taste.

‡

To ally with   art my hands partition
            the formulative prayer.
I am inclined to observe

        my old home   dusty road
bowed rain. There I will open
                if you wait patiently enough.

                    (Cultivating a silhouette
            into your lungs cosmic
                    the applause that waits).

The exhalation: tips   of elderberries promising would

        perspective flaunt.

                    Listen.

Feel   the thrush musing mouth.   The blistering

of the soft palmed   grip.
          Considered green   percussive, the killing music

          forced through me   spectacle borne catalyst.

     We are green and sick and green

and watching.

Prayer in the earth   prayer buried in soil.
The world will wait   for the revenant

          for the world   reclaims its ownership.

As if to fulminate
an incipient madness the it
inchoate

like an unextinguished
firecracker all danger to
awaken.

It is when we lose each other
in rushed-shock a union art
sickens in those afflicted

few. It is to innervate
an insurgency a dialect
of clouds.

To capture slow death
we turn to the trees
mark a zone of questionable

comfort.
How we stroke stardust
against stardust.

Blush against brutality
how pages brutalize
an endeavor.

Inexplicably we are mouthing   the law of the innocent.

   The fluxom hearts excised from our wounds.

                    The mythology is that my head remains
           stuck and porous. As wind unwinds I feel

the world shape   into parsable mechanics of words.

The whole damn bleating.

                    Toss the opening stitch   into a river

gather the effulgent cool.   This is a prayer to the Book of Perspicuity

                    of hand pressed against.

‡

                       I felt through the ether
        a longing to be enveloped.

A quick secession   lingering.
Imagine the sky

a lover. Imagine   you a shore. The distance
        that could be felt in gravity   you had location
               enough to pulse me there.

                     Let the earth
      become an affront a melodious pasture.

                Follow the   water down.

Your hands will grip enough
        to pray in star-ruptured night. Descending toward the glow
a mystic waiting.   It will braid your veins
                    drain the reflections out of you.

In a disaster the sky shakes   flashes of color.
        The wavering silence splitting   a void.

Indivisible a mirror becomes nothing
        floating in space
                skewed slightly of precept and tenant.

We will say the human mind was not made
        for precision. That words were not put there
for believing.

‡

      For here she said for here
a rippling gesticulation
      into distinct spires.
Nominative portions the falling

breaths.   The yellow and the rain
she said   the inflection
of the body altogether.

‡

A pattern roaring pulling the wind to cease.
Tonight I will choke the electrons
make the atmosphere moan.

The susurrus croaked out the silence.
I became a night of tortured footmen
their feet curled into moons.

Watch here the tumbling feather boundless
of the broken tide. The high darkness
sacrificed in flight—the storm will not abide.

‡

There was another satisfaction
furrowing into hot, slick night.
(She said pulse. Envision flare).

Sweat wicked upon atoms—
journey into awakening.

*

I spent the morning smitten,
awed in crackling melt.
The shadows winnowed like frost.
I halved into black purpose.

My security remained her exigency.
We painted our faces to attract
our charge, strangled a rapid loss.
We breathed in.

The night glowered like a polaroid
burning. From below
a trajectory bellowed
fragments—the fingers
spread thin against cool lips.

(We put life to faces, the mouths we stacked
like buildings.
Hands exploding
into duplicitous multiplicities.

When we see the world, she said
we were already being pulled
behind the reflection of a mirror—
the self was not made for excision).

‡

i put my (poetry) on you. your   skin/outshone the childish buttons
hung from knobs/of (open) doors. (the loss of) love begins/when
obsolescence (pushes silent mobs/to glom) about   conglomeration,
steal/(curvatures) (parachutes)—cohesive dubs./ in fifty-eight the river
(rose) congealed./ (your secrets) stowed (away), tattooed   and
rubbed/(onto) your skin. a kiln captures *volta*—/(the turning)   process:
metamorphosis/photography. (say *ti amo, o la/tua assenza*). say   (   )
(geneticist)./

i put my (poetry) in you. your mind/inflicted (patina—adulate) to shine.

We touch it because it's shiny and bronze and we do not understand the description in Cyrillic. We rub it because it must be good—the locals believe in action, so we mimic, because it's right. But what is the right motion, the proper pronunciation?

The proper salutation is sublime. The pocket watch is to be drawn and worn like time. Every time one might ask to measure a prolonged moment of formality. There is certainty about a man and woman dressed to stately spruce—to procure a cigarette is only a matter of asking. This gala, more than proper, is vital. Our art has manifested in the bronzed statues we have mirrored of ourselves. Twilight breaks this tie and gown affair, is broken when the sun weeps against the bloated river. This night cast in ourselves as syzygy—our bodies wrought in metal molds. In time, water will make us weep crusted memory, lest we wipe away our wear, resist the loss of all we had.

What we have shown here, our bodies sodden:

3.	thick hosts of imagery, manic spasms of constellation
4.	one time you were smacked in the face when she turned around
al.	at its furthest distance, the sky can only hold so much gravity
ao.	intrepid action salutes her with a bow
2.	strung out in victory exclamations, we fail to fall
hob.	knobbed and behind our intent, we only want to see
do.	the sea intends to claim us, the way we see it lap toward us
dob.	*hello, good sir, would you like the duck confit*
5.	i think i might be dying
aob.	sound satisfied around my discharged blood
hf.	*madam, i want to press against the bosom, refute my coldness*
df.	the water is reflective, forces us to see the image of ourselves that is fluid, motioned
7.	the openness of her flames engulfs me
hl.	i only want to know which way to the grocery store
1.	our actions before us, our chart of consequence
ho.	*repeat i think i might be dying*
af.	i felt the world wobble before me
6.	splitting us into you and me

FIG. 5.

‡

An incessant motion to connect she said to connect we need a door she said to observe a loop around the self encompassed in another self equally enormous. She said standing outside we became greener—a layer of frozen wisteria—ghosts imbued in tones curved into each other's cheekbones. She said the unfolding and recoil she said pacing the memory away. No need to create perfection. Observant I watched the silence boundary our privation—the terms sacrificing my identical cruelty. Alone—I said scatter absolve as a wreath tumbling in snow. The callous toil of perfection to make myself an entrance. Scattered indifferent catastrophe she said the semblance against she said the love we need.

‡

Nobody's there

                    as the mist ebbs out   from the frosted
           needle forest.   The evaporating dew

                held in the grass and pouring wisteria—
          so earthly damp the world just hung there.

       Night collapses,
                    a raven fluttering its escape.
                  The glint-black fullness
                      forming against a breath—
                      dense as an upwelling of bones.

Yet under the break of clouds
                         the leaves all at once
                         on the ground

and frozen like knots.

And even still, nobody's there
          until you face the threshold of forest,   where the deer cause
sudden murmuration—the slow fall of snow
                   patting the ground—
                              the brackish cry of ravens—

In this flock, you are present: who you are.

It's as if the change of seasons
                    happens instantly, even as the sun gains
               a stance
to your angled jawline.

To your angled forest line.
                          Am I there? We set out

in the moist reeds an alluvial project—
        one to collect the lacuna of stars.
        That the light from a sun could travel here   to this moment,

        that there were never obstructions

        in the empty suck of open space,
        that in a million years and more
this moment would be observable   to my tearing cold eye.

        That in a breath, a conduit of stars exists
and vanquishes

        like a sough through

        an octave of permafrost

        flickering.

The moon,
                    crossing through a crisp sky
          lifts glints of snow,
                              echoing
                    across the black mercury

pooling near the pond.

It's as if the plow of the earth
                              were a memory. We gazed away
          from gravity then back down again,
                    as a deer broke trespass
          against the murmuring, slow water.

We watched, silent, the filaments dangling,
                              the tendons splayed,
          thrashings forth—
                              the poor buck let loose
                                        a centrifugal whip.

We stood there, copse of breadth,
                    a midnight gloaming,

                              until our feet felt frozen,
                              washed with the vision
          of slight death. We turned around

                    before the crows
                              —the crickets opening the night.

‡

(Mist hovers closing us in a scene of crime.
(How did you presume my plume would endanger?)

(Have my thoughts outgrown their bodies and accumulated
in the air?)

It might be all we can do honestly to approach a sanity.

Reconciling an error in our past.
(Do you know who will ply themselves in ruptures?)

(Do you know how the light bends against us?)
Insistence

moaned in echoes, fleeting, from sky.
(There is a better gravity one that I will never contain).

Mist hovers closing us in a scene of crime).

‡

That only we wanted to survive.
That only we could arrange our eyes
toward the pillar of horses

surrounding the sun.

Imagine the smell for shame
knowing that we could have shaped our faces
        and simply refused.

                It was a matter of time

                        that the crows had any bearing—

                let me tell you I have lost everything.

Begin to think of the hue
        running down my face
in dusk.

Hemorrhaging my thoughts
a moment of quiet order.

Looming in the pasture
I prayed the prophecy

had a demeanor a swagger

we lost long ago. Pray the opening
holds questions.
The inversion of winter

rests calmly on the back

of my palm. Only these misgivings open

like a sternum of wrens.

‡

Though we bled meticulously for the portrait

fingers tethered to the moon

we could not begin to believe our trajectory

flecked pieces of our lingering lives.

The pearled abscess of the moon

ripples overspilt on the asphalt.

‡

At the end.
My body undulating   wet.
          Diaphanous

heart. Strewn   quincunx
hung from a mouth
                    it is the warmth
at the beginning   the raw
          upwelling in sharp breeze.

It is where my body ruptures.

                              The frost patterning
          a simulacra intelligence
          —spirited
          like a flower.   She clasps my arms
              squeezes   my breadth a
                                        miraculous
          snowline.   It is as if we shout
                        joy
              furiously.

‡

A crack

　　　　　　　　light

　　　　　years apart—
the dark where we cannot see.

　　　　　Let me function　　　　　a solution.
Whole world　　　　spilling.
　　　　　　　　You　　knelt me
erect my back　　　　　turned. The cold
　　　embrace you will not
forget.　　I wished for warmer days.
(You did not.　　　　　　　　)
　　　　　　　　　　Hold the breath

　　a canyon.　　　　There is
only　　the burden
　　　　　　　　　　　　　　a portrait
　　　of crumpled　　paper.
Let the day　　　　hold　　crease
　　　　　　and　　hue.
I will touch　　you there　　the solemn
　　　　　　soft of landscape bent
folding　　onto furrowed
　　　　　　　departure.

‡

...

Without the dark
ribbon in a tree, a depth of a wound.

A river jumps its banks
because this is possibility

for us both. Ourselves and yet still
connected. The fork of converging

window panes. I remain
with a perimeter of dire-hardened stares.

Understand I create a distance
of undulating wholeness.

And for the moon. I am the moon.

...

Shreds of light
through this tattered window.

I pour inside my fragile
inability to renew. My flood strokes

the tips of grass, there is frost
pooling on my fingers. I have tried.

But not enough for the thump
in you. The hollow thump

of an attic being explored.
A quill of sharpening

meadows. I am fracturing
from your mouth, the winter run

no longer feasible. Here, it is easy
to smolder. Here, the waves

folding over a grappled hold
of intimate clutches, the grips muscled

and tender. A break
of contingent trappings.

Another whorl of a world.

‡

The dance
    a wounding guilt
        upwelling from the soles
  trodden to this   spinning moment
    an energy
deliquescent.
The sun's impurities
    split into panes   of trees—
like mangled steel
a rawness of blood.

I began my reformation—late night in
the butter—buried there all confidence
quaking. I ventured to where my
outpouring became a rivulet a butterfly in
the breath. It's when sun will rise against
her skin—absent oath—imprecation
awake in the book. Obscured it is the
unsuspected menace the key before
shattering. The daring vision of a sudden
universe. In thought we had written its
limits—the page a momentum in how
we hold molecular desire suffused in
how to die.

In the aftershock, a forest trembling.
And you, here, kudzu, wrapping

    your want   on every errant limb.

‡

(The morning opened outward like two palms
separating a virtue.
There were tonally two birds surrounded
by hundreds of onlookers, a tree
on fire yet yearning to be halved.
(The changing face
of a rested moon). A fury of splinters
strewn on the ground like lackadaisical
despair. This is how the air ends. Toiled
with fresh forests the rain
just before fissure.
(There are motes of collapse,
a silence still promised). Then a deer
emerged from the pit in my chest).

Martyr in the breath.
Martyr in thumping.
Let your face blacken.

‡

When my body latched
onto its trajectory
I felt the phthisis
drain from my skin,   torso to fingertip,
like a cauldron of mud   glowing past its compression.

That gravity contained in itself   unknowably a minuteness
grasping—an unfurling
flower. The bend of stem   a promise
to kiss the ground.

‡

And away, an illegible
        wind
—lost context of shape.

            Pure energy and echoing white.   Voluminous
        not understanding   my feet digging

        in a semblance of gravitational sway

—how easy it is to turn
and see my arrival.   Yet

                    The haptic transmits a sense of being
                    swallowed. Her cutaneous echoing. In her I
                    foraged a recovery. Blank like a face left blank.
                    A sculptor's neck rough in incompletion.
                    In her the grid of streets was a map to new
                    love and new erosions of myself. In her I let
                    my flocks wander. The mind and its masks
                    became confessions to greater infidelities.
                    Growth became a callous on my bones. In
                    her I let indiscreet scars mark a history of
                    recapture. All those risks we took to love.

        my bearings like a tree dropping roots.
                        I cannot

see my next step
            as if the sun were
            shattered by a blanket

                    hewing a distance around my feet.
(Only in moments
when a body flounders in crisis).

‡

                        We find trauma   in responding
to corporeal shadows—   pleas that kill   in snowfall—

        Rifted other a plea that   can be forgiven a plea

            the rotting body   owns its abscess

                                            to those
                        who forget to swallow a future.

Parallel of prayer   a plea
                    the hands balled into seizure.
          The hearthy warm
as if the instant   is internal viscosity

          hands cannot shake loose—drop of honey
     from cloud to shuddering

                    plea's nape. Sweet benediction—
          body bowed in humiliation—

                    as if the body would collapse upright.
          The jaw
would linger as flies
                    explode from the depths
          of my chest like a sullen cough.

     In the book my ink is made of ashes.
               My last portrait hemorrhaging

the liquefaction of my body
transmutes conquest
searching out its weight
like a meticulous recoil
expansionary
in pounding soil.

‡

There, a universe about to burst—
the panic, the midday tonguing, an alibi in each
language we've found. We pretend to comprehend the vigil

      (yet we do not know)
      where *solitude* outpaces *immensity.*

      in truth, the mountain always looms
      no, the outcome of prophecy.

We place the echo in the mouth
and in the stitches before our interdict,
we practice wearing our pasts and try to speak.

                        Last night, her mouth opened.
                        I want to know what it meant,
                            its insistence on tournament.

                In mythology we find moldered rhymes—

            We remember the mouth on the mountain
                    and go there to cast out our origins.

‡

Still, in another life. Some things
are water spots on my writing
     the way I say burn the mountain,
     create an invention of murmurs,

     you posing for an erasure—
     how language never feels quite full

Held like water, the sparrow folding into its own,
edgeless, she manipulates the control.

And one thing is for certain: I was not dying,
yet I was not accustomed
        to flight. The high omission of death
halve the day, unplant the world.

        Our silenceable memory
        we have been shaping to open

        In summer, the mountain has a tone.
        When she says *repeat the bloom*
                I pour out generations.

‡

About ferocity. As if the day floods
like a burgeoned river. The action of nothing
is a violence against my opening vision.

The mountain claims its gravity
in water. My preoccupation in self-fulfilled prophecy.
Next time, I swallow the valley.

Tragic the consequence of movement. The pulsar manipulations

drowning the future. Say here is one road where the revenant

bleaches in sun. In sun   there is a cowardice of fixity tracing

ancient questions in the imprints of my stride. A call to death. Let the blur

be the burrow into my fractured pile of reminiscence: the benefaction of

my journey. The leafing frost departing on traveler's jaws.   The

breakage of the genuine savior the meadow a backdrop to telemetry.

Towers for days.   It is by chance we echo across the canopy of a

familiar sky. My madness is the memory where I began to flee.

The road as it ever was a harbinger   the frozen captured

parts of deer strewn across a mile. In sun the faultless warming of the

traveler's perpetual breath. In sun   visions   of   heat-

pounded shadows slowly erupting and all at once the traveler in and

around the desolate BOOK OF MISCONCEPTION. Here the world

slants   it refrains from scarcity in sun it positions the traveler toward

mirrors of deserts. Desolate becomes the examination pardoned

in reason. I must have a voice but it is not there   in   sun   I am cloaked in silence. Simulated and fraught saguaro melodium. We place our ears to the apocalypse. The return to horizon a parallax impulsion a mystery I once swam among. How much have I already forgotten? How much did we never know? Let the owls hum where the horizon cracks a creature with five faces. The fourth face is a prayer in the distance of hope and recollection. The fifth a Darwinian mask history revealed in defective orbits.   More important the absence of face in death. That which becomes forgotten or as particular as sands in desert. A stand-in for whole corpse. Apologia in apostrophe. The first three despair silently inescapable like an oxen-hooved tract of expansive solemnity. Creature you are the traveler and likewise a stone. Creature in sun you are the evacuation. The BOOK OF RELENTLESS MOANINGS foretells of landscapes peeling like meat from bone. In sun the sun in sun. There can never be any misconception. The traveler will return to returning. No the traveler will not return. There can never be clemency for absences traverse ages of feet and fields.   I could never misremember how I pled goodbye:

heavens pushing in sun mapping a conciliatory prayer for movement.

The voice a kind of music   facing the inability to breathe. O

against the tabernacles of morning the prayer spilt to deny markings on

roads. Half in moon half placed in our veins invocation of anathema

stilted backdrop of godspeed. But the road is here in the surface-

tinged pallor   placed neatly in the BOOK. Let the moon be

a moaning. A fragile   atmosphere to lose. In sun the moon splinters

from the world the action succedent to remembering supplicant powers.

The revenant becomes a prayer   the traveler despaired of

relentless sun. The road bends crooked and forms bodies with land. In

land sun diverts catacombs succumbing to combed out teeth. The body

prays subversive if in sun the path encumbers a spirit within us. O sun

unearth my hardened reason the day I sickened my duty. O forceful

deception! The calyx of morning   reveals a creeping cistern a

collection that cannot be severed from my mind. Have I poisoned my

memory? Chosen I am forced to subsist on velleity   the earth opening

its atmosphere to place sun upward against the revenant's finger.

I have tried every night to forget your infamy but cast new vowels to curse. Distillation of cellmate to foot the reactive cacoethes my dreams chisel in particular angles of rocks. The trial of lifespan to harden a solecism   in swagger. In sun preternatural asphyxiation preoccupied in right motion. THE BOOK OF SHADOWS foretells that necessary reactions to solitude do not end in gazes toward Western plains. Action my hero the lonely self   pry time into a passage of chants.   An elusive seizure of the body's ineffable hum. How utterance assuages   dictions within truly   coincidental sun I have forgotten the brutality we endeavor. In sun pageantry lives in dire preservation. Passenger the sky to blister. That flying reflects

in ways too near the heart. The body will not be interrupted. From a dry creek the world molders so hard.   The foot's art a path to pretense a child rupturing into thousands of blossoming flowers the brilliant remnants of what may thought to have existed. In sun the wake pulls my delivery   the sound of songs quaking from our feet. To have existed is to explode   in the folds of life. The purity wastes us context relents. Orange textures create a rift of measurable

absence in breakage. Here my wonderment begins. In firm words I set

upon a journey—incorruptible I with my we will always say your name

as flowers burning. Your memory in sun is the matter-of-factness crows

have sheened into malleable identities. In sun shadows mark a passing

of self onto people the threshold THE   BOOK   calls   to   question.

Imagination in the right dark sky. We speak the path smelt-historied

present a perfectly   heartbreaking endurance   a   furtively

arduous book. Barren perfect crumbling of trajectory of motioned

palms. A prayer pleading for a shred of night.

‡

Dear She the last

    reconciliation.

An assemblage

    fasting. It is day
    again and the herons
wade slowly confronting
the familiar tarn.
    Fastening a rotor
to the engine, a convenience
      defamiliarized of sweat.

Mine is wooden.
It rots on its edges.

    The heron still
cautious confronting
    an unknown mirror
    no more a mirror
than its unknown face

no one undone.
Life tearing its seams

like the knots we tie
to each other's hands
      undoing always a slip
      or tightening at the very
resistance of love.

‡

In an alterity   the harvest falls

like a blackened sea. The sweeps
        of beginnings subcoital   and fused.

Lingering remnants   teased out
        accreted like electricity

the cold nether sweat

she has.

‡

The horizon scrawls itself
    terminally,   consummates an alacrity

     she might sing.

     What is the day
     what is a blizzard

to come back from?

                    Subinflectual a corrigenda

     of body between sun.

‡

I fusiform on
to I beneath the haptic
in this reality the predilection
am becoming.

She said an almost

I to intonation. Wavering exile
the singing upon singing

positioned such to hone the lamb   underground

sub-sea
sub-cutonic

caterwaul of crisis upon the almost
she said

blurred into being   horizon
          scrawled terminally like a tattoo

                    of ionic charge shedding its love
                              its particular thoroughness.

The atomic ground all miniscule ministry

the force becoming   precise minuteness—

          threading aesthetic preference

                              to skin being shed
          body to body mouth to
                    body to hemorrhaging still.

                              All the dirty laments
          I want to do.

‡

As if the pith uncoiled
masterfully this renaissance.

‡

Splayed into   my sweet referent

        my catatonic referent   nor I

    not here not groveling   a fatal launch

            hem to hemlock the questioning of
            where did the sun arrive

        in her irises, those densely blue charcoaled
                        filaments I said "of a heart

        I must learn to unmake."

The bestial inside the bevy
        floundering between aphasia and not knowing

                we knew everything   in the particles
            around us—   put it there
                and remember.

                    A presence blazes

        pre-science—
    and compression, the imperfect, mythology

    to chasm—moaning   underwater   moaning.

‡

Like an extended arm
                    the shaking quiver of wrist—
        injected errata
                    filaments I have known in drowning.

                        Encased "I" becomes inappropriate
            we that proprioception
                    intransigent—

                                in dual attraction we seams
                    strong—stable

I say "When thunder is the dilettante
                the dialectical reaction, the body lingers

                            gaunt malapropria—
                    carefully committed to
            instability atomic bonds about to break.

            It is when we wavers

                the parenthetical
                        bleeds into knowing—
Apostrophic mantra
        epileptic astronomy—

                    we cannot know we
                        and where we are becoming.

(Such is an observation

a foray into negligence.
Without the dark philanthropy

we may not know our selves

outlined in ecstatic portraits.

Indiscretion a part of me
but maybe, too, of you,

Reader. In this, you are culpable
the very image of my friend.

Do not listen to mea culpa.

Feel who you have become

and may be meadowing.

Motionless, propagate a pattern
a combatant in my mouth I want

to speak you so badly).

‡

"Glacial mistakes have happened" she said,
turning, celebrating, "And before
we could melt"

"Infatiguable the horizon
                    weeps for you, for me"

☦

Debtor in acrimony home
                                    all the way. Say we say it
as if erotic the tension belongs
             in our legs. Home all   the way. Perilous

crescendo—interwoven blood
           extracts vitality in perfunctory task.
                      Cautious minuet. Instinctive nasal vibrancy.
                         Glottis sounds wetcontained.

                Home   all the   way.

        A single wave single
—amorous virtue all the way
in a single sine.

‡

Fidelity that thing.

‡

                              Engaged that broken task
              reduced   to piecemeal. A whole

                  shattering visible as if   put together.

                                                Function

        its spilling.

                      It   is what we find when outloud

  a feeling recoils.   That through hell

                  a large portion determines the outpouring

                              –hatched.

                        Effloresces into it.
        We say the name and forget the virtues

                                  that virtually we inhabits—
                                  in portraits

                                  it is unnamed the infedility

        that we
                refuses to parlay.

‡

That we couldn't say we
as in—was connected.

(Lost as such ideas leave

verily either full

or half nothing. We sang the middle
of excision. That home   is the numb drunk.

We are not-melting the failure
that we could not

salvage a veil
in this winter mud. Instinctively
(yes we couldn't say we because it didn't exist)

permanence had become an object
like the gin-well and covet-green.
and we felt

reconciling
we stored in profanity).
Home all the way.

‡

It ends abruptly—percussive aphasia—but how we define it is a tidal
forest. The ebb

all around how we am growing black gardens, thick pools of shadows
til they bloom. It lurks
like the trips planted in time.
Tell we that it will be broken, resolved, rather revolved, in evolution—
that is, it growing despite its growth, that hairy
lump of it.

It becomes a new undertow, which nearer the flower may drift, we
never can recede
until it precedes a rift.
That caterwauled coral, dried on our nape.
The safety weeping distance.

It's that we will never
find a home to share,
obstinate we, seaweed hooked we in branches,
the idea that we
as individuals,
could pattern the very surface of the moon—
that wretch of a moon—
it pulls we in torpor, in late mornings,
the very callous mark of infinity,
how small we can see.

‡

Forgive me   for coming home
        alone. For the tufts

                of culture greased in my hair.

        That alone the world recalls

            and spins, spins and spins.

‡

We set out   no not it
        not the it we had become.

                We as separated calamity but we

                        knew not the fingers   scraping beneath
        the skull.

As if we could fall into perimeters
                        and not say it like the rest of we.

                Here   we am saying it—
                        we found erratic warmth
                in the cold winter.
        Not a promise yet it sustains.

                It became a notion   of precise mantra.

Hope in the future. Hope in the yaw. Hope all around we could not see.

        In the warm breast   of the gull it moves us further

                to a station blackening the in-between.

ACKNOWLEDGEMENTS

Thank you to the editors of the following journals, where excerpts of THOUGH WE BLED METICULOUSLY originally appeared: *alice blue review, Caketrain, Deluge, Dreginald, Handsome, jubilat, Small Po[r]tions, Timber* & *Yalobusha Review.*

Gesture diagram is from Albert Bacon's *A Manual of Gesture* (1875). Collapsible revolving door diagram is from U.S. Patent No. RE14255 to Theophilus Van Kannel, issued February 6, 1917.

Thank you to Emileigh Barnes, Zachary Carlsen, Carl Corder, Brett DeFries, Michele Finkelstein, Rachel Finkelstein, Ossian Foley, Jane Gregory, Kate Rutledge Jaffe, Burke Jam, Torin Jensen, Ashby Kinch, Genevieve Kohlhardt, Julia Madsen, Caryl Pagel, Colin Post, Peter Richards, Alison Riley, Karin Schalm, Ed Skoog, Nick Twemlow, Karen Volkman, Jeff Whitney, and Jane Wong, for your support, time, and friendship. Special thanks to Janaka Stucky, Carrie Olivia Adams, A. Minetta Gould, Nikkita Cohoon, and everybody at Black Ocean for publishing this book.

Indelible gratitude to Daniel D'Angelo, Joanna Klink, Elizabeth Robinson, Prageeta Sharma, and Dale Sherrard for your incredible attention and insight to this book and its ideas.

Thank you to the following places for your space and inspiration: Butterfly Herbs, The National Portrait Gallery and American Art Museum, Hirshhorn Museum (particularly for the Damage Control exhibit), and Frontierspace.